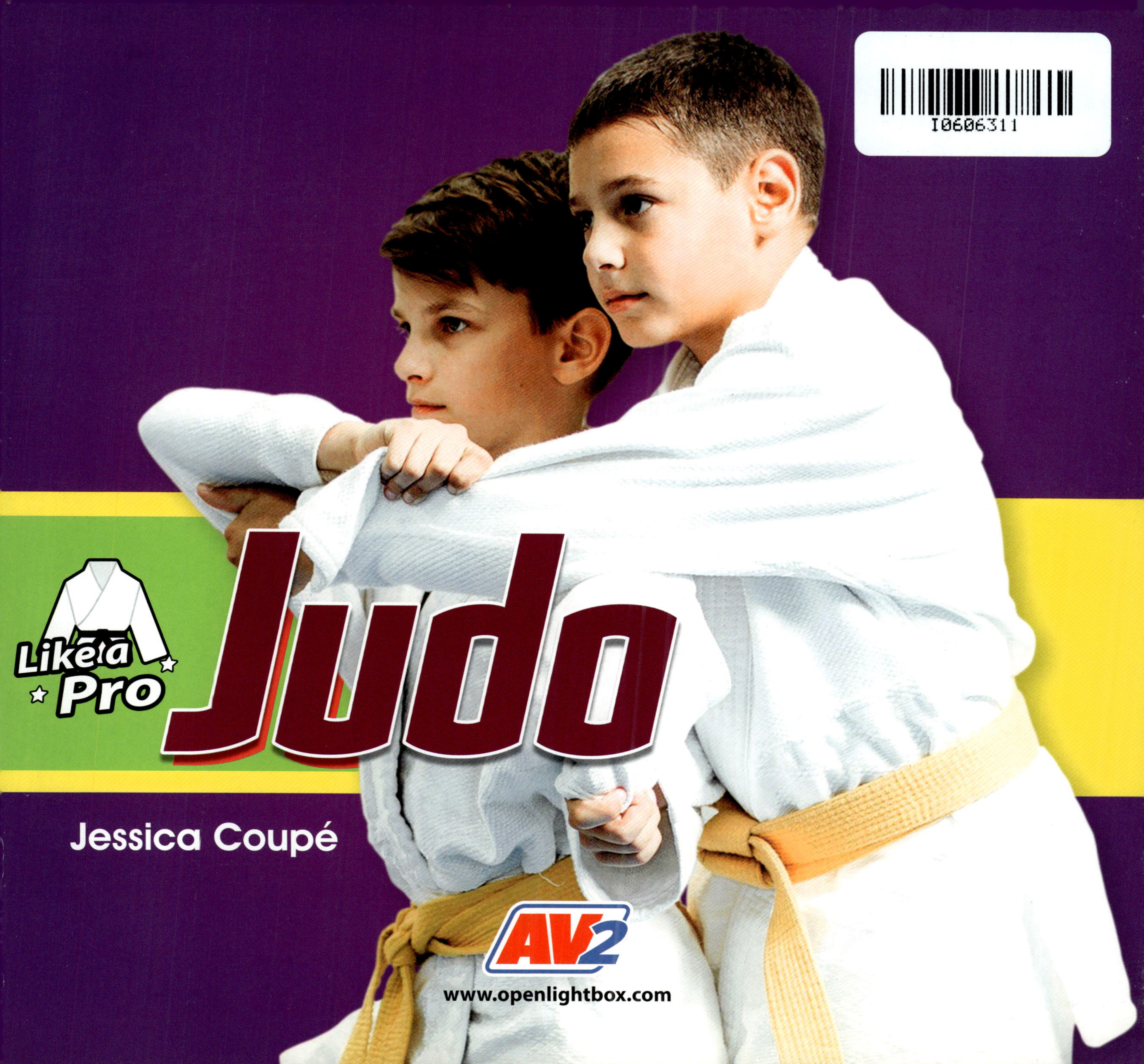

Like a Pro
Judo
Jessica Coupé
AV2
www.openlightbox.com

Step 1
Go to **www.openlightbox.com**

Step 2
Enter this unique code

ZCFMJCLJI

Step 3
Explore your interactive eBook!

AV2

Judo

Start!

AV2 is optimized for use on any device

Your interactive eBook comes with...

Audio
Listen to the entire book read aloud

Videos
Watch informative video clips

Weblinks
Gain additional information for research

Try This!
Complete activities and hands-on experiments

Key Words
Study vocabulary, and complete a matching word activity

Quizzes
Test your knowledge

Slideshows
View images and captions

Share
Share titles within your Learning Management System (LMS) or Library Circulation System

Citation
Create bibliographical references following the Chicago Manual of Style

This title is part of our AV2 digital subscription

1-Year K–5 Subscription
ISBN 978-1-7911-3320-7

Access hundreds of AV2 titles with our digital subscription.
Sign up for a FREE trial at **www.openlightbox/trial**

Contents

I love judo.
I am going to
do judo today.

Judo began more than 100 years ago.

I get dressed for judo. I wear my uniform. It is called a judogi.

Judo wrestlers must follow a strict dress code.

I am new to judo. I have a white belt.

Judo experts have black belts.

I go to a building called a dojo for judo practice.

There are mats on the dojo's floor. There is a safety zone and a playing area.

I warm up before I practice. I stretch so that I am ready.

Pro judo wrestlers practice several times every week.

At the dojo, I stand across from another wrestler.

We bow to each other. Then, the match starts.

I try to throw the other wrestler down on the mat.

If the other wrestler falls on the mat, I win the match.

Sometimes, my dojo competes against other dojos.

The team that wins the most matches wins the event.

I love judo.

BRITISH
JUDO

JUDO FACTS

These pages provide more detail about the interesting facts found in the book. They are intended to be used by adults as a learning support to help young readers round out their knowledge of each sport featured in the *Like a Pro* series.

Pages 4–5

Getting Ready Judo is a sport in which two people wrestle. It was created in Japan by Dr. Jigoro Kano. It is based on jujitsu. Dr. Kano changed elements of jujitsu to make it safer. The word *judo* means "the gentle way." In judo, people are not allowed to kick or punch each other. They try to gain control of the other player with special wrestling techniques. Judo wrestlers are called judokas. The goal is to throw the other wrestler onto the mat. Millions of people worldwide practice judo.

Pages 6–7

What I Wear Each judoka wears a uniform called a judogi. It is a loose jacket, made of thick material, worn with pants. The judogi needs to be durable so that it does not rip easily. A belt is wrapped around the jacket. It is tied with a traditional knot. Beginning judokas receive white belts. As their skill increases, they earn different colored belts. Experts wear black belts. Judokas participate in their sport with bare feet.

Pages 8–9

What I Need Students do not need much equipment to participate in judo. They might want to have a bag to carry their judogi. Many students bring a water bottle and a snack to practices as well. Some judokas wear pads to protect their elbows and knees. Professional judokas may wear mouthguards to protect their teeth when wrestling. Some tape their ankles to protect them as well.

Pages 10–11

Where I Play Judo matches are played in a building called a dojo. In the dojo are special mats called tatami, used to ensure the comfort and safety of the judokas. The mats are two different colors. The safety zone is one color, while the playing area is another. The playing area is a square. It is between 26.25 by 26.25 feet (8 by 8 meters) and 32.8 by 32.8 feet (10 by 10 m). Dojos often contain exercise equipment. These tools help judo students learn balance and strength.

Pages 12–13

Warming Up Warming up before practicing or competing in a match helps prevent common judo injuries. There are several warm-up exercises judokas may do. Common warm-ups get the blood flowing, stretch joints, and strengthen the stomach and back. The exercises also help judokas with agility. Students roll forward and backward. They stretch their legs and arms, do push up and sit ups, and stand on one leg. Students also do exercises that strengthen their core muscles. These muscles help with stability.

Pages 14–15

Playing the Game A judo wrestling contest is between two people. One person wears a white judogi, while the other wears blue. The referee invites them to stand opposite each other. The contestants bow to each other before and after the match to show humility and respect. A match lasts 3 to 5 minutes. During that time, each judoka will try to throw the other on his or her back on the mat. Judokas use various judo moves to accomplish this. They do hip and shoulder throws or try to sweep each other onto the mat with their feet.

Pages 16–17

Winning the Game A referee assigns points and penalties. Points are given based on certain holds. To win a match, a judoka must score more points than the other. Judokas that throw their opponent so that they land on their back on the mat score an ippon, winning the match. Players may also earn points called waza-ari for lesser holds. A judoka with two waza-aris also wins the match. Judokas receive penalties if they break the rules.

Pages 18–19

Team Play Judo first became an Olympic sport in 1964. Judo teams are made up of six players, with three men and three women. Each judoka competes in a match against someone of about the same weight from the other team. After all matches are complete, the team with the most wins is victorious.

Pages 20–21

I Love Judo Judo is fun and has many health benefits. One major focus of the sport is self-improvement. Judokas try to improve their skills to earn the next belt. As they practice these skills, they build physical strength. This includes muscle strength and heart health. Judo also helps participants learn to focus and treat others with courtesy and respect. Judokas should eat healthily. Eating fruits, grains, and vegetables provides energy.

KEY WORDS

Research has shown that as much as 65 percent of all written material published in English is made up of 300 words. These 300 words cannot be taught using pictures or learned by sounding them out. They must be recognized by sight. This book contains 45 common sight words to help young readers improve their reading fluency and comprehension. This book also teaches young readers several important content words, such as proper nouns. These words are paired with pictures to aid in learning and improve understanding.

Page	Sight Words First Appearance
4	am, do, I, to
5	a, began, like, more, than, years
6	for, get, is, it, my
7	follow, must
8	have, new, white
10	go
11	and, are, on, the, there
12	before, so, that, up
13	every, times
14	another, at, from
15	each, other, starts, then, we
16	down, try
17	if
18	sometimes
19	most

Page	Content Words First Appearance
4	judo
5	pro
6	judogi, uniform
7	dress code, wrestlers
8	belt
9	experts
10	building, dojo, practice
11	floor, mats, playing area, safety zone
13	week
15	match
19	event, team

Published by Lightbox Learning Inc.
276 5th Avenue, Suite 704 #917
New York, NY 10001
Website: www.openlightbox.com

Library of Congress Control Number: 2022934156

ISBN 978-1-7911-4851-5 (hardcover)
ISBN 978-1-7911-4853-9 (softcover)
ISBN 978-1-7911-4852-2 (multi-user eBook)

042022
100921

Printed in Guangzhou, China
1 2 3 4 5 6 7 8 9 0 26 25 24 23 22

Project Coordinator: John Willis
Designer: Jean Faye Marie Rodriguez

Every reasonable effort has been made to trace ownership and to obtain permission to reprint copyright material. The publisher would be pleased to have any errors or omissions brought to its attention so that they may be corrected in subsequent printings.

The publisher acknowledges Alamy, Getty Images, and Shutterstock as its primary image suppliers for this title.